Safety Rules

- Always prepare with an adult present

- Use age appropriate potion bottles/cups

- Add edible ingredients only inside the potion bottle/cup

- Consume immediately. Storage not recommended.

- PARENTS: Review ingredient labels for each recipe. Ingredients listed here may include dyes and other common food allergens. *Substitute as needed for your child.*

Spellbook of Spooky Potions

J.L. HOLDEN

Potion Bottle
Decoration Supplies

- Craft store potion bottles or small plastic cups
- Spooky themed candy
- Tea stained labels
- Spooky stickers
- Googly eyes
- Cauldron for mixing
- Spider webs, twine, charms
- Craft putty and paint

For ghosts and goblins toil and trouble pour a little Witch's Bubble

1 packet lemon-lime drink mix
2 cups Pineapple Juice
2 cups lemon-lime soda
1 container Lime Sherbert

Witch's Bubble

Prepare drink mix as directed

Add pineapple and soda to drink mix

Pour liquid mix over sherbert when ready to drink

1 box lemon-lime jello
1 box strawberry jello
strawberries

**Prepare jello as directed
(or use prepared jello cups)
In a mixing bowl
add jello and strawberries
roughly chop mixture**

1 gal Blue punch
32 oz Sparkling Water
Ice

Mix berry blue
punch and
sparkling water
Add crushed ice

2 liter Grape Soda
48 oz vanilla ice cream

Pour grape soda over vanilla ice cream when ready to serve

2 liter Cherry Soda
1 cup Pineapple Juice
1 container Lime Sherbert

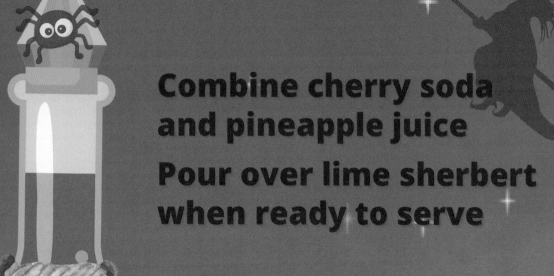

**Combine cherry soda
and pineapple juice**

**Pour over lime sherbert
when ready to serve**

1 cup Limeade
1 cup Pineapple Juice
1 cup Blue Juice

**Combine limeade,
pineapple juice and
blue juice
Add crushed ice**

POTION

MONSTER MASH

1 gal Red Punch
2 ltr Lemon-Lime Soda
Strawberry Syrup

Combine punch and soda
Add syrup to taste for
a thicker consistency

1 pack Instant Hot Chocolate
Whip Topping
3 Chocolate cookies
Halloween Themed Marshmallows

Prepare hot chocolate as directed
Add whip topping
Crush cookies and layer over whip topping
Garnish with Halloween themed marshmallows

My Magic Potion:

_____

_____

_____

_____

_____

_____

_____

_____

The
end

Printed in Great Britain
by Amazon

33203647R00016